Dehydrator Cookbook

TABLE OF CONTENTS

INTRODUCTION

Food dehydration is an ancient method of preservation still in existence today. It has proven to be an effective way of prolonging the shelf life of foods such as veggies, meat, fruits, etc. It reduces the weight and volume of food, making it easy to transform into backpack meals, especially meals that can be restored to its original form just by adding water. It also helps you create the homemade version of tasty meals with desired flavors that are not sold in stores.

While dehydration is perhaps the oldest method of food preservation, it is still a very effective method used in today's world. And with the use of equipment such as the food dehydrator, it becomes an easy task to practice and enjoy. The whole idea of dehydration is to take away moisture from the food and prevent spoilage. This process happens through concurrent heat transfer for evaporation to the meal and water vapor removal from the meal.

This cookbook discusses at length all you need to know about food dehydration. It simplifies the recipes for you to understand and practice easily. You also find information on choosing the right dehydrator and tips to keep in mind when dehydrating your meals. More importantly, the recipes in this book are broken down in steps so you can have the same result or even better results if you decide to get creative with your desired flavors.

With the right equipment and the right measurement, you can have so much fun while dehydrating your favorite meals. This book gives you the basic information you need to get started, and if you confidently try out all that has been said in this book, you will begin to dehydrate like a pro in no time. Enjoy!

CHAPTER 1: DEHYDRATING 101

Dehydrating is a cost-effective method of processing fresh foods for storage. This method of food processing can preserve foods for indefinite periods by extracting moisture from the food to suppress the growth of microorganisms. Dehydrating removes water content from foods through low heat and steady airflow.

The tools required for dehydration vary with different food products. Contrary to what some individuals assume, dehydrating foods keep in most of the nutrients. This means that you still get the benefits that you would normally get if you ate the food while it was fresh. Another benefit of dehydrating food is that it allows you to control your nutritional profile. Although there are several backpacking meal options available in stores, not many of them are tasty. If your nutritional need is different from the available options, dehydrating your meals allows you to control the final product, whether you want a recipe with less salt or gluten-free – you can make it how you want it. To dehydrate your meals, the best equipment to use is a food dehydrator. This kitchen appliance uses a light flow of hot air to extract moisture from foods and dry them to prevent spoilage.

How to Choose a Suitable Food Dehydrator

Basically, there are two categories of food dehydrators; Vertical Flow Dehydrators and Horizontal Flow Dehydrators. Other than their orientation, these two categories of food dehydrators work differently.

The vertical type of dehydrator is affordable, but it does not spread the heat uniformly. This makes it good enough for veggies and fruits but requires additional effort to dehydrate meat effectively. When using this type of dehydrator, it's essential to keep in mind that it doesn't heat as evenly as a horizontal food dehydrator and also to make a habit of switching out trays to achieve the best results.

On the other hand, horizontal flow food dehydrators are quite expensive, but they spread heat more uniformly throughout the equipment. This makes it the best choice for dehydrating meat or for making beef jerky. It is also arguably the easiest appliance to use. All you have to do is get the appliance started and continue to relax until your food is ready. They are also ideal for processing tougher vegetables and for trying out challenging recipes.

Consider the following when choosing your food dehydrator:

1. **Size and Capacity:** It's essential to let your preference match the purpose of use.

2. **Price:** You should also consider the price and how easy it is to operate. The presence of a timer in a dehydrator makes it convenient to use. You can easily get it started, and it will alert you when the food is completely processed

3. **Noise:** The fan in some models produce noise while working.

4. **Temperature:** Consider the fact that different foods dry under different temperatures - this makes it crucial that the thermostat on your device is adjustable.

Dehydrating Tips

It's essential to note that not all foods dehydrate well. There are certain foods that should be avoided as much as possible for safety reasons. These foods include; avocados, olives, fats, and dairy products. Dehydrating these foods tends to result in food poisoning or affect the shelf life of the final product.

It's also crucial to dehydrate foods at the correct temperature. If the temperature is too high for the food, it could result in food hardening. Likewise, if the temperature is too low, it could result in bacterial growth, which defeats the whole purpose of dehydrating in the first place. A general guideline for temperature control when dehydrating foods include; 165°F for Poultry; 160°F for Meat and Seafood; 135°F for Fruit; 145°F for Grains and Meats (pre-cooked); 95°F for Herbs; 125°F for Veggies, Beans and Lentils.

Another tip to keep in mind when dehydrating is to avoid turning up the heat when trying to speed up the process. If you wish to speed up the dehydrating process, you can slice your food into smaller pieces, reduce the thickness or reduce the food load in your dehydrator.

When getting your equipment and food ready for dehydrating, ensure that all surfaces and tools are clean and dry. As much as you can, cut your food into uniform pieces, pretreat the necessary foods to retain their color, flavor, and overall shelf life. However, note that not all fruits or vegetables require pretreatment.

Storage of dehydrated food

A well-dehydrated food can last for months, and in some cases, as long as a year. Nevertheless, the shelf life of dehydrated food depends on the dehydration process and the method of storage. You can store your dehydrated foods in airtight containers, vacuum sealing bags, resealable containers with refrigeration, and also Mylar Bags with an oxygen absorber. The whole point of dehydrating is to remove moisture from the foods. That means wherever you choose to store your foods should meet certain conditions. These conditions include keeping the foods away from light, oxygen, and moisture. It's also essential to allow the food to cool completely before transferring them from the dehydrator into the chosen storage condition.

Rehydrating Dehydrated foods

There are three methods you can use when rehydrating your dehydrated foods. If your storage container is a mylar bag, one of the methods you can use is simply adding boiling water to the mylar bag and allowing it to rehydrate. This method may take time, but it is the cleanest and most efficient.

Another method of rehydration is to add the dehydrated food in a pot containing water and allow it to soak for a little while. Afterward, simmer the food until it is rehydrated. This method does not take as much time but uses the most fuel.

The last method is similar to the second one, but the difference is that; after soaking for a while, cover up the pot and simmer the mix for a few minutes before removing from the heat. After removing from the heat, let the food rehydrate with a pot cozy but remember to stir after about ten minutes—a general rule when rehydrating is to use equal parts water to food. But you can always add more water if required. You can also add extras such as cheese to the food.

CHAPTER 2: FRUITS

Apple Chips

Yield: 6 Serves

Total Time: 8 hours 10 minutes

Ingredients:

- 2 fresh ripe organic apples
- ½ tbsp ground cinnamon
- ½ tbsp granulated sweetener (optional)
- ½ bowl lemon juice

Instructions

- Prepare your apples by cleaning and cutting off the stem part of the apples. Use a Mandolin or a sharp knife.

- Slice the apple uniformly into thin rounds of ¼ inch thickness
- Remove the seeds, and if you wish, you may remove the peels also.
- In a bowl, combine the lemon juice and cold water. Stir gently.
- Transfer the sliced apples into the bowl containing the lemon-water mix for about 60 seconds. Stir gently to ensure the apples are well-coated
- Completely drain the apples. Then, transfer the drained apples back into the bowl.
- Mix the sliced apples with the ground cinnamon. If needed, you may add any granulated sweetener of your choice.
- Arrange the sliced apples, preferably in a single layer, on the trays of your food dehydrator. Set the temperature to 135°F.
- Allow drying for about 8 hours.
- Store in airtight containers.

Cucumber Chips

Total Time: 8 hours 10 minutes

Yield: 12 serves

Ingredients

- 4 cucumbers
- 4 tablespoons olive oil or vinegar
- ½ teaspoon chili powder
- ½ teaspoon paprika(smoked)

Instructions

- Preheat your dehydrator, set the temperature to 130°F
- Clean your cucumbers and slice them uniformly. Use a mandolin or sharp knife.
- Mix the slices in four tbsp of olive oil. You can replace olive oil with vinegar.
- Arrange the coated slices carefully on the dehydrator tray and sprinkle the chili powder and paprika on your sliced

cucumbers. Ensure to leave space between the cucumber chips.

- Transfer into your pre-heated dehydrator and dehydrate for about 10 hours or until your cucumber chips are dry and crisp.
- Allow the chips to cool and transfer into an airtight container for storage.

Pliable Dehydrated Peaches

Total Time: 34 hours 30 minutes

Yield: 5 serves

Ingredients

- 1 ½ tbsp vinegar
- 3 lbs. ripe peaches
- 4 cups of water

Instructions

- In a bowl, mix the vinegar (you can use lemon juice as a substitute) with water. Put the mix aside.
- Blanch the peaches by soaking in a bowl filled with boiled water for 60 seconds. Then transfer into another bowl containing water and ice.
- When chilled, remove the peaches and peel off their skins. The skins should remove easily or use a paring knife.

- Use acidulated water solution to prevent discoloration of the peeled peaches.
- Depending on the type of peaches you're dehydrating (freestone or clingstone), pit and cut them into wedges of about ¼ inch thickness.
- Transfer the sliced and pitted peaches back into the water solution. Then drain them in a colander.
- When they are well-drained, transfer the slices onto the dehydrator trays.
- Ensure there's enough space between the slices (about an inch or ½ inch space)
- Adjust your dehydrator temperature to 135°F
- Allow the peaches to dehydrate for about 30 - 34 hours (this can be lesser depending on the thickness of the sliced peaches.
- When testing for dryness, allow the peaches to cool off for about half an hour after turning off your dehydrator.

- The result should feel pliable. Transfer them into airtight containers for storage

Chewy Dehydrated Bananas

Yield: 8 serves

Total Time: 8 hours 15 minutes

Ingredients

- 10 lbs. Bananas
- 1 cup lemon juice

Instructions

- Start by peeling the bananas. Ensure you use ripe bananas.
- Using a mandolin, slice the banana uniformly in a tray to about ¼ inch thickness.
- Transfer and spread the sliced bananas on the tray of your dehydrator. Avoid overlapping the slices.
- Set the temperature to 135°F. Dehydrate for about 7 - 10 hours. The timing varies as a result of the difference in humidity. A rule of

thumb is to stick around for the last 3 hours to check the level of doneness.

- Store the dehydrated slices in airtight containers, enjoy.

Dehydrated Cherries

Yield: 8 Serves

Total Time: 17 hours 45 minutes

Ingredients

- 1 lb. Sweet fresh cherries
- ½ tbsp lemon juice

Instructions

- Thoroughly wash the cherries and pit them.
- Fill a bowl with the lemon juice. Place the pitted fresh cherries in the bowl and ensure they are well coated.
- Fill the trays of your dehydrator with the cherries and ensure they are well-spaced.
- Dehydrate the pitied cherries for about 18 hours.
- When you touch the dehydrated cherries, they should feel slightly tacky.
- Transfer them into airtight containers.

Dehydrated Strawberries

Yield: 1 ½ cups for every round

Total Time: 6 hours 10 minutes

Ingredients

- 1 lb. strawberries

Instructions

- Use 1 pound of fresh strawberries per tray.
- Rinse the berries thoroughly. Slice them into rounds of about ¼ inch thickness.
- Set the dehydrator temperature to 135°F and dry the fruits for at least 6 hours.
- When done, allow to cool and store in tightly sealed containers.

CHAPTER 3: VEGETABLES

Crunchy Broccoli Chips

Total Time: 12 hours

Yield: 6 serves

Ingredients

- 2 ¾ lbs. Broccoli
- 4 tbsp tamari sauce (low sodium)
- 4 tbsp yeast
- ½ cup hemp seeds (optional)
- ½ cup of vegetable broth or water
- 2 garlic cloves
- 2 tsp onion powder

Instructions

- Cut the broccoli into florets, place them into a mixing bowl, and put aside.
- Place yeast, cloves, tamari sauce, onion powder, vegetable broth/water, and hemp seeds in a blender or food processor and puree until smooth.
- Add the sauce mix to the bowl containing the florets. Toss together carefully until florets are well-coated with the sauce.
- Transfer the florets to a parchment paper or silicone dehydrator sheets and dehydrate for 11 hours. Dehydrator temperature should be set at 115°F.
- The resulting chips will be crunchy when they are well dehydrated.
- Store in airtight containers

Onion Powder

Total Time: 6 hours 15 minutes

Yield: ¼ cup

Ingredients

- 4 fresh onions

Instructions

- Cut the onions into thin ring slices of about ¼ inch thickness
- Place the onion rings on the dehydrator trays. Ensuring enough space is not as important as it is for other recipes. This means your onion rings can overlap, and you'll still have a great result.
- Turn on the dehydrator and set the temperature to 135°F
- Dehydrate onions for 5 or 6 hours.
- The dehydrated result will be dry and brittle.

- Using a good food processor, blend the dehydrated onion to the desired degree of consistency.
- Store the onion powder in tightly sealed containers.

Chili Pepper Powder

Total Time: 5 hours 10 minutes

Yield: 10 Serves

Ingredients

- 1 lb. chili pepper pods

Instructions

- Choose fresh chili peppers pods, wash them gently and pat dry.
- Remove the pepper stems and slice the pods accordingly. If the pods are thick, slice them into rings; otherwise, just cut them in half. Remember to wear hand gloves while doing this.
- When transferring the sliced peppers on the dehydrator trays, remember to spread them out as evenly as possible to encourage uniform heat distribution.

- Turn on the dehydrator and set the temperature to 135°F. Dehydrate for about 5 hours until dry.

- Blend the dehydrated peppers to your desired consistency. Let the powder sit in the blender for about 10 minutes before opening to avoid inhaling the hot spice.

- Store the pepper powder in tightly sealed containers.

Carrot Crisps

Total Time: 7 hours 10 minutes

Serves: 8 serves

Ingredients

- 2 carrots
- ¼ teaspoon salt
- 1 tablespoon coconut oil
- 1 teaspoon cinnamon

Instructions

- Rinse the carrots thoroughly and slice them thinly into a mixing bowl.
- Add salt, cinnamon, and coconut oil. Mix to coat the carrots.
- Spread the coated carrots on the dehydrator trays.
- Allow drying for about 5 - 7 hours until crispy. Allow the dehydrated chips to cool.
- Store in airtight containers.

Sweet Potato Chips

Total Time: 20 hours 15 minutes

Yield: 4 Serves

Ingredients

- 2 sweet potatoes, sliced thinly
- sea salt to taste

Instructions

- Using a mandolin, slice the potatoes as uniformly and thinly as possible.
- Add salt and toss with the sliced potatoes. Spread the slices on the dehydrator tray, ensuring they are in a single layer.
- Turn on the dehydrator and set the temperature to 115°F.
- Dehydrate for 15 - 20 hours.
- Store the chips in airtight containers.

Zucchini Chips

Total Time: 12 hours: 15 minutes

Yield: 8 Serves

Ingredients

- 8 medium zucchinis
- ½ cup apple cider vinegar
- salt to taste
- pepper to taste
- chili powder to taste

Instructions

- Using a mandolin or knife, slice the zucchini uniformly into rounds of ¼ inch thickness.
- Place the sliced zucchini in a bowl. Add salt, pepper, chili powder, and apple cider vinegar to the bowl.
- Toss the ingredient together to coat the zucchini slices. Make sure you separate any pieces that stick together.

- Spread the zucchini slices on your dehydrator trays. Avoid overlapping the slices and dehydrate for 10 – 12 hours at 135°F.
- Store the crispy chips in airtight containers.

CHAPTER 4: LEATHERS

Strawberry Rhubarb Leather

Yield: 3 – 6 Serves

Total Time: 6 hours 15 minutes

Ingredients

- 4 cups rhubarb
- 6 cups strawberries
- ½ cup honey

Instructions

- Rinse the fruit thoroughly. Remove the stems and dice the strawberries and rhubarb.
- To soften the diced rhubarb, transfer them into a pot, add a little water, and cook until soft over medium heat.

- Using a food processor, puree all the ingredients (including the cooked rhubarb). You may replace the honey with any sweetener of your choice.
- Set the dehydrator temperature to 145°F. Line the dehydrator trays with parchment paper and spread the mixture thinly and evenly on the parchment paper.
- Dehydrate for 6 hours or until leathery. Allow cooling before removing from the dehydrator.
- Roll the leather and cut into desired lengths with a sharp knife.
- Wrap the pieces and store them in airtight containers.

Blueberry Chia Banana Leather

Yield: 4 – 6 Serves

Total Time: 8 hours 15 minutes

Ingredients

- 4 cups blueberries
- 4 small ripe bananas
- ½ cup chia seeds
- 10 - 15 dates (pitted)

Instructions

- Wash the berries and bananas. Remove the stems and pits.
- Put all the ingredients in a food processor and blend until smooth.
- Line the dehydrator trays with parchment paper and spread the mix thinly and evenly on the parchment paper.
- Set the dehydrator temperature to 145°F and dehydrate for 6 - 8 hours or until leathery.

- Allow cooling before removing from the dehydrator.
- Roll the leather tightly and cut into desired lengths with a sharp knife.
- Wrap the pieces using saran wrap and store them in airtight containers.

Raspberry Leather

Total Time: 4 hours 10 minutes

Yield: 8 Serves

Ingredients

- 4 cups fresh raspberries
- 6 tablespoons white sugar
- 1 lemon

Instructions

- Juice the lemon and blend the juice in a food processor with the raspberries and sugar.
- Line the dehydrator tray with parchment paper. Spread out the raspberry-mix evenly across the dehydrator tray.
- Turn on the dehydrator and adjust the temperature to 140°F.
- Dehydrate for at least 4 hours until the raspberry leather no longer feels sticky when touched.

- When cool, cut into desired lengths with a sharp knife. Roll up in parchment paper or wrap with saran wrap and store in an airtight container.

Mango Lime Leather

Total Time: 12 hours 5 minutes

Yield: 2 rolls up

Ingredients

- 8 cups of mango (about 4 mangoes)
- 12 tbsp freshly squeezed lime juice (from about 6 limes)
- 2 cups applesauce
- ½ cup honey or add needed

Instructions

- Wash, peel, and chop the mango.

- In a blender, combine the mango, honey, applesauce, and freshly squeezed lime and puree. Taste the blended mix and add honey as needed. Ensure the mix is not too thick.

- Line the dehydrator trays with parchment paper. Spread out a thin layer of the mango mix on the dehydrator trays.

- Set temperature to 135°F and dehydrate for 12 – 18 hours. Note that the timing may take up to 20 hours in some cases. But when the leather is done, it would be non-sticky.

- Allow the leather to cool and cut into strips before storing them in airtight containers.

CHAPTER 5: CHIPS

Beet Chips

Total: 8 hours 30 minutes

Yield: 8 Serves

Ingredients

- 6 large beets
- ½ cup of water
- ½ cup apple cider vinegar
- 2 tbsp olive oil
- 2 tbsp sea salt flakes

Instructions

- Peel the beets and cut them into thin slices using a mandolin or a knife. Place the sliced beets into a bowl.

- Add the remaining ingredients except for the sea salt flakes to the bowl. Allow marinating for about 15 minutes.
- Transfer the beets to the dehydrator trays, arranging them in a single layer. Sprinkle the salt flakes on the beets and dehydrate for 8 hours at 135°F.
- Store in tightly sealed containers.

Sriracha with Garlic Kale Chips

Yield: 6 Serves

Total Time: 5 hours 10 minutes

Ingredients

- 2 bunches curly kale leaves,
- 4 tbsp nutritional yeast
- 2 tbsp dried Sriracha
- ½ tsp garlic powder
- 1 tsp sugar
- 3 tsp kosher salt
- 4 tbsp olive oil

Instructions

- Separate the kale leaves from the stems by hand-tearing them into chip-sized pieces. Wash the leaves thoroughly and dry them using a clean towel.
- In a mixing bowl, toss together the sriracha seasoning, garlic, sugar, yeast, and kosher salt.

- In another sizable bowl, coat the chip-sized leaves with olive oil. Then, add the seasoning mix to the bowl of kale leaves. Mix together to coat well.
- Spread out the coated kale leaves on the dehydrator trays, arranging in a single layer. Avoid overlapping.
- Turn the dehydrator on and set the temperature to 115°F.
- Dehydrate for about 5 hours or until crispy.
- Allow to cool and store in airtight containers.

Ranch Carrot Chips

Yield: 8 – 10 Serves

Total time: 9 hours 10 mins

Ingredients

- 8 carrots
- 2 tbsp ranch seasoning
- Salt to taste
- pepper to taste
- lemon juice or water (optional)

Instructions

- Rinse the carrots thoroughly and cut them into thin slices using a mandolin.
- Transfer the sliced carrots into a bowl. Sprinkle with ranch seasoning, pepper, and salt to taste.
- Use the lemon juice or water to make the seasoning stick if your carrots are too dry.

- Arrange the slices on the dehydrator trays. Ensure you space the slices and set the temperature to 115°F.
- Turn on the food dehydrator and dehydrate for 8 hours or until firm and crunchy.
- When cool, store the crunchy carrots in an airtight container.

Plantain Chips

Total Time: 3 hours 5 minutes

Yield:

Ingredients

- Himalayan pink salt
- Cinnamon
- Plantains

Instructions

- Peel the plantains and cut them uniformly into thin circular pieces.
- Transfer the sliced plantains to the dehydrator trays. Sprinkle salt and cinnamon on the chips.
- Adjust dehydrator temperature to 135°F and dry for 3 hours or until done.
- Store the chips in a tightly sealed container.

CHAPTER 6: MEAT JERKY

Ground Beef Jerky

Yield: 12 Serves

Total Time: 8 hours 10 minutes

Ingredients

- 1 ½ lb. lean ground beef
- 2 tsp salt
- 2 tsp smoke flavor
- 1 ¼ tsp black pepper
- 2 tsp garlic (dried and minced)
- 2 tsp onion powder

Instructions

- Break up the beef in a sizable mixing bowl and sprinkle the remaining ingredients on it.

- Mix up the ingredients until blended and keep in the refrigerator overnight.

- Set the dehydrator temperature to 145°F when you're ready to dehydrate and remember to line the trays with parchment paper.

- Pack your jerky gun with the meat and squeeze out lines of meat according to your desired length on the trays in your dehydrator.

- Dehydrate the ground beef for about three hours before checking for doneness. Shuffle the trays if required to ensure even distribution of heat.

- Continue to dehydrate for additional 4 – 5 hours until the beef jerky is done. Clean off any grease and leave them to cool off.

- You can store in the refrigerator or seal in airtight containers.

Venison Jerky

Yield: 8 Serves

Total Time: 28 hours 15 minutes

Ingredients

- 2 pounds venison roast (thinly sliced)
- 8 tbsp coconut aminos
- 8 tbsp Worcestershire sauce
- ½ tsp black pepper
- ½ tsp garlic powder
- ½ tsp teaspoon onion powder
- ½ tsp pepper flakes
- 1 tsp sea salt
- 2 tbsp honey

Instructions

- Prepare your venison by removing the skin and refrigerating for 60 minutes.
- Cut the meat into thin slices of about ¼ inch thickness.

- In a non-reactive bowl, mix the red pepper flakes, Worcestershire sauce, black pepper, onion powder, coconut aminos, honey, and sea salt.
- Add the slices of the jerky to the bowl, ensuring that the slices are well-coated with the marinade.
- Cover the mixing bowl and refrigerate for about a day or two while the venison marinates.
- Afterward, remove the marinated jerky from the refrigerator and place it on cooling racks to drain off the meat.
- Arrange the meat slices on your dehydrator trays, ensuring there's enough space between them.
- Set dehydrator to 160°F and dehydrate for about 4 hours.

- To test for doneness, bend the strip. If it cracks without breaking, it means the jerky is done.
- Store the jerky in vacuum seal bags or Ziploc bags.

Lamb Jerky

Total Time: 36 hours 15 minutes

Yield: 4 Serves

Ingredients

- 100g lamb loin
- 4g original bacon cure
- chili flakes
- lime
- cracked rainbow pepper
- mixed herbs
- Jerk seasoning
- Indonesian long pepper
- caraway

Instructions

- Start by cutting the lamb loin, put it in a bag, and coat it with the bacon cure. Ensure the bag is well-tied before refrigerating for a day.

- After about 24 hours, your lamb should look pink. If it's not, that means it needs more curing time.
- Transfer the lamb to a tray and cut into the middle of its largest part.
- On the cutting board, add your seasoning ingredients. You can add flavorings if you want. Roll the meat in the ingredients for even coating.
- Arrange the prepared meat in your dehydrator trays, ensuring they are in a single layer.
- Adjust your dehydrator temperature to 115°F and allow it to dry for 12 – 13 hours.
- When testing for doneness, the lamb jerky will snap on its grain and not just bend. It needs another dehydrating hour if the meat bends at this stage.

- When done, remove the lamb jerky and allow it to cool for about 60 minutes before storing in tightly sealed bags or containers.

Teriyaki Beef Jerky

Total Time: 18 hours 10 minutes

Yield: 4 Serves

Ingredients

- 1 pound top round beef
- ½ tbsp sesame oil
- ¼ cup of soy sauce
- ⅛ cup brown sugar
- ½ clove garlic
- ⅛ cup pineapple juice
- ½ tbsp sesame seeds
- ⅛ tsp ginger

Instructions

- Prepare the meat by cutting it across the grain into slices of about 1/5-inch thickness.
- In a bowl, mix up sugar, oil, freshly grated garlic, sesame seeds, soy sauce, and pineapple juice.

- Transfer the marinade into a Ziploc bag with the top round beef and refrigerate overnight (about 12 hours) or for a day.

- Afterward, drain off the beef and discard the marinade.

- Transfer the marinated slices to your dehydrator trays and adjust the temperature to 165°F.

- Dehydrate for 6 more hours or until done.

- When done, allow to cool and store in airtight containers.

Carne Seca Jerky

Total Time: 6 hours

Yield: 2 pounds

Ingredients

- 4 lbs. beef brisket
- 2 dried Anaheim
- 1 tbsp sea salt
- 2 limes

Instructions

- Trim the brisket and cut against the grain into slices of about ¼ inch thickness. Place in a bowl and set aside.
- Prepare a skillet and toast the chile in it for about 30 seconds per side. Remove stem and seed from the chile when cool.
- Break the chile pods into pieces and grind into a fine powder of desired consistency.

- Add the chile powder to a bowl and mix it with the fine sea salt.

- Add the chile-salt mix to the sliced beef brisket. Squeeze the lime juice over the beef and toss it all together to coat the beef as evenly as possible.

- Cover up the bowl and place it in the fridge for 3 hours or more.

- Set the sliced meat on your dehydrator racks. Ensure there's no overlapping.

- Set your dehydrator temperature to 145°F and dehydrate for 2 – 3 hours. You may have to shuffle your dehydrator trays to ensure a uniform dehydration process.

- When done, the sliced beef will be firm yet pliable.

- Allow the beef jerky to cool before transferring into a covered container that allows a bit of airflow.

CHAPTER 7: SEAFOOD

Dehydrated Shrimp

Total Time: 7 hours

Yield: ½ quart

Ingredients

- ½ lb. shrimp (shells on)
- Water
- ¼ cup kosher salt

Instructions

- Add the kosher salt to about ½ quart water. Ensure the salt dissolves completely before submerging the shrimp in the brine. Leave for about 5 hours, or better still, leave overnight.

- If you prefer, you may smoke your shrimp for a couple of hours with the smoker at a temperature of 180°F.

- To dry your shrimp, set dehydrator temperature to 135°F. Transfer the shrimp onto the trays and dehydrate for an hour before adjusting the temperature to 110°F. Dehydrate for about an hour more or until the shrimp snaps in half cleanly when you bend it.

- When done, turn off the dehydrator and allow the shrimp to cool to room temperature. Then, transfer to an airtight container.

- If you wish, you may store in a silica pack desiccant to prevent water build up in storage.

Salmon Jerky

Total Time: 16 hours

Yield: 4 - 6 Serves

Ingredients

- Salmon fillets
- 2 cup salt (not iodized)
- 5 cups light brown sugar
- ½ cup of soy sauce
- 8 quarts water
- Cayenne pepper (optional)

Instruction

- Combine soy sauce, sugar, and water in a big pot.
- Over medium heat, bring the pot to a boil, frequently stirring till the sugar dissolves. Remove the pot from the heat and allow cooling (preferably to room temperature).

- Cut the salmon fillets (with skin removed) into strips. Transfer the strips into the brine mix and refrigerate for about 10 hours.

- Drain the salmon and discard the marinade. Rinse the salmon with clean water and let it drain. When drained, use paper towels to dry the salmon.

- Prepare your dehydrator by spraying the trays with vegetable oil. Transfer the salmon strips onto the trays, ensuring they are arranged with enough space between them.

- If you desire, sprinkle cayenne pepper on the strips to taste. Set temperature to 135°F or according to your equipment's recommendations.

- Dehydrate for about 8 hours or until your desired doneness.

- Store the salmon jerky in an airtight container or sealed Ziploc bag.

Dried Prawn Crackers

Yield: 6 Serves

Total Time: 10 hours

Ingredients

- 4 lbs. prawns
- 4 lbs. tapioca starch
- 9 tsp salt
- 8 tsp sugar
- 4 tsp pepper
- water

Instructions

- Make sure the prawns are rinsed, peeled, and de-veined. Pat dry with a kitchen towel before processing it in a food processor. Process until it becomes a paste.
- Transfer into a sizable bowl and toss in the salt, sugar, pepper, and tapioca starch. Mix thoroughly until well combined. You may

69

transfer into a stand mixer and use the dough hook to knead and smoothen the mix.

- Prepare a greased plate, roll the kneaded paste into 1 ½ inch logs, and place on the greased plate. Cover the plate with a piece of foil (greased as well).

- Put water in a pressure cooker up to an inch. Place a stand to raise the plate above the water. Then, put the covered plate into the cooker and cook for half an hour.

- When cooked, wrap them in foil after cooling. Transfer into the freezer to harden the prawn paste.

- Using a sharp knife, cut the paste thinly into slices. Arrange the slices on your dehydrator tray and dry them at 135°F for about 4 hours or until the desired doneness.

- Store in a tightly sealed bag or airtight containers.

Scallop Chips

Total Time: 16 hours

Yield: Half pound

Ingredients

- 9 oz. scallops

Instructions

- Put the scallops in a Pacojet beaker and place it in the freezer. When frozen, process the scallops on a pacojet into an ultra-fine texture (slightly sticky)
- On silicone mats, spread the scallop paste, dividing the brushstrokes into fields of 6 by 8 cm.
- Transfer the silicone mats into the oven at 122 °F (40% wind cycle with the air shutter opened). Remove the scallops when they start to let go of the mats.

- When removed from the oven, cut around edges on each scallop chip using scissors.
- Set the scallop chips onto your dehydrator trays and dry at 104°F for about 4 hours.

Trout Jerky

Total Time: 6 hours 15 minutes

Yield: 2 serves

Ingredients

- ½ cup soy sauce
- 2 tbsp brown sugar
- 2 tsp olive oil
- 2 tsp minced garlic
- 1 tsp freshly ground black pepper
- 2 lbs. trout fillets (cut into 1-inch wide strips lengthwise)

Instructions

- In a saucepan, add minced clove, soy sauce, light brown sugar, olive, and black pepper. Toss the ingredients together and place the saucepan over low heat.
- When the brown sugar is gently melted, remove immediately from heat and allow the

mix to cool completely back to room temperature.

- Cut the trout fillets lengthwise into strips of about 1-inch thickness. Put the strips in a plastic Ziploc bag and cover it in the cold marinade.

- Remember to squeeze the air out of the bag before closing it tightly. Refrigerate for 6 or 8 hours.

- After refrigerating, transfer the strips into a sizable strainer and let all the juices drip for about 6-7 minutes.

- Use paper towels to dry each fish strip afterward and prepare your dehydrator. Arrange the strips on the dehydrator rack without touching or overlapping.

- Set the temperature to 135°F and dehydrate for 4 hours or a jerky setting.

- When done, the jerky will have a leathery and chewy texture. Turn off the dehydrator and allow the jerky to cool for 30-60 minutes. Store in airtight containers.

CHAPTER 8: JUST ADD WATER MEALS

Chili Corn Chips

Yield: 3 Serves

Total Time: 12 hours 30 minutes

Ingredients

- ¼ cup quinoa, uncooked
- ½ tablespoon olive oil
- ½ onion, diced
- 3 minced garlic cloves
- 1 can diced tomatoes
- ½ (8 oz.) can tomato sauce
- ½ can diced green chilies (optional)
- 1¼ tablespoons chili powder
- 1 teaspoon cumin

- 1 teaspoon cacao powder
- 3/4 teaspoon smoked paprika
- ½ teaspoon sugar
- ¼ teaspoon coriander
- salt to taste
- Pepper to taste
- ½ (7 oz.) can corn, drained
- 1 (10 oz.) can kidney beans, drained & rinsed
- ½ (10 oz.) can black beans, drained & rinsed

Instructions

- Cook the quinoa according to given directions and set aside.
- Place a big pan over medium-high heat and add oil.
- Add the diced onions to the hot oil and cook until tender. Then, stir in minced garlic.
- Add the cooked quinoa into the pan with tomato sauce, cumin, coriander, cacao

powder, diced tomatoes, chili powder, and sugar.

- Then, season with salt and pepper to taste. Add the diced green chilies and bring the mix to a boil.

- Afterward, reduce the heat and simmer for about half an hour, stirring frequently.

- Stir in the beans and corn and continue cooking for 15 minutes. Allow cooling before dehydrating.

- Line the dehydrator trays with parchment paper and set the temperature at 145°F.

- Dry the mixture for about 10 hours or overnight.

- When done, allow to cool to room temperature and seal in vacuum bags. Refrigerate until you're ready to use it.

- Portion mini tortilla chips or grain crackers in small bags to go with each serving.

To rehydrate

- Just add about 1½ cups of boiled water to the mixture in a pot. Place in a cozy for a few minutes until well-rehydrated.

- Stir and add more water, if required. Enjoy with tortilla chips or grain crackers.

Dehydrated Pasta Carbonara

Yield: 2 Serves

Total Time: 6 hours 20 minutes

Ingredients

- 2 cups pasta (pre-cooked & dried pasta)
- 2 oz. chicken (dried)
- ¼ cup peas (dried)
- ½ teaspoon parsley (dried)
- ½ teaspoon paprika
- ½ teaspoon garlic powder
- 1 teaspoon salt
- 1 teaspoon black pepper
- Parmesan cheese
- Butter or oil

Instructions

- Pre-cook the pasta and steam the frozen peas. Also, pre-cook your chicken.

- Set dehydrator temperature to 160°F and dehydrate the chicken, pasta, and peas for 6 hours or until dry.
- Combine them in a snack bag. Combine the remaining ingredients in a separate sizable plastic bag or use a tightly sealed container for longevity.

To rehydrate

- Add about 4 cups of boiled water to a bowl. Add in all the ingredients except the butter and cheese.

- Ensure water is just above the meal in the bowl. If the water is much, drain off the excess. Allow the meal to sit for 15 minutes in a cozy to be well-rehydrated.

- When the water is absorbed, add the butter and cheese. Stir to combine and enjoy.

Ready Spaghetti

Yield: 2 Serves

Total Time: 24 hours

Ingredients

- 1 cup pre-cooked and dried pasta
- ½ cup ground beef (dried)
- 50g dried sauce
- 50g dried vegetables (onion, green peppers, and mushrooms)
- Breadcrumbs, as needed
- Italian seasoning

Combine the following separately in snack-size bags:

- Parmesan cheese (dry)
- Oil or butter (optional)

Instructions

- Set your dehydrator temperature to 135°F. Pre-cook the pasta and dehydrate for 4 hours.

Also, dehydrate the spaghetti sauce at the same temperature for 6 hours.

- Dice and saute the onions. Then dehydrate together with the green peppers and mushrooms at 135°F for 5 hours.

- Then, cook the lean ground beef. Drain off the fat, mix with breadcrumbs, and Italian seasonings. Stir the mixture occasionally while dehydrating at 160°F for 8 hours. Combine all in a plastic bag.

- In separate bags, store the dry parmesan cheese and oil or butter (if using).

To rehydrate

- Boil about 3 cups of water and transfer into a bowl. Add in all the ingredients except oil and cheese.

- Mix and allow to sit in a cozy for 15 minutes until well-rehydrated. When the water is absorbed, add the cheese for improved texture and oil if you desire. Enjoy.

Mexican Burrito

Yield: 2 Serves

Total Time: 6 hours 20 minutes

Ingredient

- 1 cup dried beans
- 50g dried chicken
- 50g instant rice
- 50g dried salsa, low sodium
- ½ teaspoon chili powder
- ½ teaspoon garlic powder
- ½ teaspoon onion powder
- ½ teaspoon cumin

Instructions

- Rinse the beans thoroughly. Set the dehydrator temperature to 160°F and dehydrate the beans for 6 hours. Also, dehydrate the chicken at the same temperature for 6 hours.

- Dice and cook the veggies and dehydrate them with salsa.
- In a plastic snack bag, combine all the ingredients.

To rehydrate

- Add 3-4 cups of water to a bowl. Toss in all the ingredients and mix well.

- Allow the meal to sit in a cozy for 15 minutes until well-rehydrated. Check to see if more water is needed or drain if in excess.

- Enjoy when all the water is absorbed.

Mac and Cheese with Turkey

Yield: 2 Serves

Total Time: 7 hours 5 minutes

Ingredients

- 2½ cup pre-cooked & dried macaroni noodles
- 2/3 cup dried turkey breast
- 1 tablespoon powdered butter (optional)
- 1 tablespoon powdered milk (optional)
- 1 powdered cheese packet or 6 tablespoons cheese powder

Combine the following in a separate snack-size bag:

- Bread crumbs
- Oil (optional)
- Parmesan cheese (dry)

Instructions

- Slice your smoked turkey breast thinly into strips and dehydrate the strips at 160°F for 6 hours.

- Pre-cook about one box of macaroni noodles and dehydrate.

- Combine the dehydrated noodles and turkey in a plastic bag.

- Pack breadcrumbs, oil, and parmesan cheese separately in a snack-size bag.

- Combine the rest of the ingredients in a plastic bag.

To rehydrate

- Boil about 3 cups of water and transfer into a bowl. Add the dried macaroni and turkey. Ensure the water is just above the meal.

- Allow sitting in a cozy for 15 minutes until it's well-rehydrated. Drain any excess liquid and pour the noodles and turkey back into the bag.

- Heat about 6 tablespoons of water and stir in butter, milk, and cheese powders to make the cheese sauce.

- Mix the cheese sauce with the noodles. Drizzle oil over the mixture or add butter if you desire. Top your meal with the breadcrumb-parmesan mix.

Dehydrated Pad Thai

Yield: 2 Serves

Total Time: 14 hours 12 minutes

Ingredients

- 12 ounces rice noodles
- 2 green onions (chopped)
- 50g dehydrated chicken (optional)
- ½ cup of powdered eggs (freeze-dried)
- 2 tablespoons cilantro (freeze-dried)
- 2 tablespoons oil
- 4 packages of soy sauce
- 2 tablespoons sugar
- 2 teaspoons lime powder
- 2 tablespoons unsalted peanuts (chopped and roasted)

Instructions

- Chop the green onions and dehydrate at 135°F for 10 hours or overnight. If you wish to add chicken, adjust dehydrator temperature to 160°F and dehydrate it for 4 hours.

- Combine the dehydrated onions, dried chicken, and rice noodles into a gallon Ziploc bag.
- Add the freeze-dried eggs and cilantro into a snack-size bag.
- Put the remaining ingredients in a separate snack-size bag.

To rehydrate

- Fill a pot with water and boil. Carefully pour the hot water into the Ziploc bag.

- Ensure the ingredients in the bag are fully submerged. Allow it to sit for about 10 minutes and set aside.

- In the meantime, add about 6 tablespoons of water to the powdered eggs. In your pot, heat the 2 teaspoons of oil and scramble the eggs until firm.

- Soak noodles in water until soft. Drain off the water, add in the scrambled egg, and place it aside.

- Heat the remaining oil in the pot and add in soy sauce, lime, and sugar. Stir to combine the sauce, then stir in the noodle mix to coat. Top the meal with peanuts, enjoy.

Chimichurri Chicken with Rice

Yield: 2 Serves

Total Time: 6 hours 30 minutes

Ingredients

- ½ pound canned chicken
- 4 tablespoons of chimichurri seasoning
- 1 cup of dried shrimp
- 2 cups cooked instant rice
- Olive oil

Instructions

- Set dehydrator temperature to 160°F and dehydrate the canned chicken for 6 hours.
- Combine all the ingredients into a Ziploc bag, except the olive oil – it should be in packets or place in a small bottle.

To rehydrate

- Boil about 3 cups of water and transfer into a bowl. Stir in the olive oil, seasoning, shrimp, chicken, and the rice.

- Stir and leave for about 10 minutes or until well-rehydrated. Adjust the water level if required and enjoy it.

Tom Yum Soup

Yield: 2 Serves

Total Time: 6 hours 30 minutes

Ingredients

- 2 Tom yum bouillon cube
- 2/3 cup shrimp (dried)
- 3 tablespoons mushrooms (sliced and dried)
- 3 tablespoons tomatoes (diced and dried)
- 1 onion (chopped and dried)
- 2 teaspoons dried cilantro
- 2 cups instant rice

Instructions

- Slice the tomatoes and mushrooms, and then chop the onions. Set dehydrator temperature at 135°F and dehydrate for 6 hours.
- Combine 3 tablespoons of the dehydrated mushroom, 3 tablespoons of dehydrated tomatoes, and 3 tablespoons of onion to a

Ziploc bag. Add the remaining ingredients into the bag - the instant rice should make about 3 cups of cooked rice.

To rehydrate

- Just add about 5 cups of boiled water to a bowl. Add in all the ingredients packed into the Ziploc bag and stir. Leave for about 15 minutes in a cozy until well-rehydrated.

- The meal is ready when the rice and veggies are soft. Enjoy.

Curried Cashew Couscous

Yield: 2 Serves

Total Time: 6 hours 30 minutes

Ingredients

- ½ cup dried vegetables (peas, carrots, etc.)
- 1 cup couscous
- 2 tablespoons coconut milk powder
- 1 ½ curry powder
- 2 chicken bouillon cube or powder
- 1 teaspoon dried cilantro (optional)

Combine in a separate snack-size bag

- ½ cup golden raisins
- ½ cup cashews
- oil or butter (optional)

Instructions

- Pack golden raisins and cashews in a snack-size bag. And if using, pack butter separately.

- Thaw, steam, and dehydrate the vegetables in the dehydrator at 135°F for 6 hours or until dry.
- Combine the dehydrated vegetables and the remaining ingredients in a Ziploc bag.

To rehydrate

- Add about 2 ½ cups of boiled water to a bowl, add the mix in the Ziploc bag to the water, and stir. Allow sitting for 15 minutes in a cozy.
- When it's well-rehydrated and all the water is absorbed, add butter or oil (optional) to enhance the taste. Top it with the cashews and golden raisins.

OTHER BOOKS BY HOLLY KRISTIN

Ayurveda Cookbook

https://mybook.to/HollyKristinAyurveda

Baked Donut Cookbook

http://mybook.to/hollykristinbakeddonut

Pressure Canning Cookbook

https://mybook.to/HollyKristinCanning

Mediterranean Diet Cookbook

https://mybook.to/HollyKristinMedDiet

The Easy AIP Diet Cookbook

https://mybook.to/HollyKristinAIPdiet

Rheumatoid Arthritis Cookbook

http://getbook.at/hollykristinrheumatoid

Canning & Preserving for Beginners

https://mybook.to/HollyKristinPreserving

The Essential Wood Pellet Smoker and Grill

Cookbook

https://getbook.at/woodpelletcookbook

Made in United States
Troutdale, OR
11/18/2023

14709780R00063